CW01467433

AUSTRIA'S
BEST-KEPT
SECRETS UNVEILED

Discover 50 unique
and hidden treasures

Dieter J. F. Haselsteiner

ISBN: 9798327466746

INTRODUCTION

Travel improves the mind and clears away our prejudices.

Oscar Wilde

Having lived in Austria for around 40 years, having grown up in Lower Austria next to the river Danube and close to Vienna, I became aware very early about Austria's richness in every aspect. Austria's diverse nature, culture, history as well as people make the country a traveler's favorite choice in many aspects. With this book I dedicated my experience, my feelings and relationship with this beautiful country I would like to share with you. Come a long on this wonderful journey to explore 50 unique opportunities and insights about a small country with a big heart.

Enjoy reading!

Dieter J. F.

Content

Experience Vienna: The Unforgettable Highlights of the Danube Metropolis

Welcome to Vienna, the majestic capital of Austria, which captivates visitors from around the world with its rich history, cultural diversity, and unique charm. Immerse yourself in the vibrant heart of Central Europe and discover the unforgettable highlights that Vienna has to offer. Due to its abundance of historical landmarks, Vienna is often referred to as a living museum. The density of architectural marvels, each with its own unique story, makes Vienna truly special. Despite the seemingly endless list of highlights, allow me to list my top 5 attractions that are definitely worth exploring during a visit to Vienna:

Begin your Vienna exploration with a visit to the magnificent Schönbrunn Palace, once the summer residence of the Habsburgs. Explore the opulent Baroque gardens, stroll through the splendid rooms of the palace, and enjoy the breathtaking view over the city from the Gloriette. In addition to its imperial history, Schönbrunn Palace can be wonderfully combined with the nearby Schönbrunn Zoo, one of the oldest zoos in the world.

An absolute must-see is the imposing St. Stephen's Cathedral, the symbol of Vienna, located in the heart of the city. Admire its Gothic architecture and explore the winding streets of the old town, lined with historic buildings, charming cafes, and traditional shops.

A contrasting experience awaits you in the amusement world of the Prater, Vienna's most famous amusement park. A highlight is the historic Ferris wheel, from which you can enjoy a spectacular view of the city.

Marvel at masterpieces by famous artists at the Kunsthistorisches Museum, one of the most significant art collections in the world. From Renaissance paintings to Egyptian artifacts, the museum offers a fascinating journey through art history.

Experience the unique Viennese coffee house culture in one of the traditional cafes and savor the delicious coffee specialties and sweet treats. Also, enjoy the diverse Viennese cuisine, from hearty Wiener Schnitzels to delicate Sachertorten.

To fully immerse yourself in Vienna, I recommend taking your time and exploring the city on foot or by bicycle; the compact structure of the city makes it possible.

Hospitality with Sensitivity: The Tipping Culture in Austria

Austria is renowned beyond its borders for its coziness and hospitality. But what about tipping here? Firstly, it's important to note that tipping in Austria is a voluntary gesture and not obligatory. While tipping is not mandatory in Austria, it is still appreciated and is a way to express your satisfaction or appreciation for the service. In restaurants and cafes, it's customary to round up the bill amount. There isn't a set percentage or rule. Staff members appreciate it when you round up to the next two to five euros, depending on the number of guests served.

It's worth mentioning that splitting bills is common in Austria, and you don't have to settle a total bill per table. Leave the tip either directly on the table when paying or preferably hand it directly to the staff, as this brings the most joy. When using a taxi, you can also round up the fare. Similarly, for other services like hairdresser visits or tour guides, it's common to give a small tip to express your gratitude. The same goes for craftsmen and similar services.

You can be sure that tips will be acknowledged with a smile and may even lead to further conversations or helpfulness. If you're ever dissatisfied with the service, it's perfectly fine not to leave a tip.

Diversity as the Foundation of Austria's "Colorful" Population

The population of Austria has a complex origin that traces back to a long history. Historically, Austria has been a melting pot of various peoples and cultures, including Celtic, Roman, Germanic, and Slavic influences. Over the centuries, these influences have been shaped by migration, wars, and political changes, resulting in a unique cultural diversity. The Habsburg Monarchy, which ruled for centuries, had a significant impact. It was a mosaic of different peoples and ethnicities united under a common empire, each maintaining its own languages, cultures, and traditions. Furthermore, the Austro-Hungarian Monarchy, also known as the "Dual Monarchy" or "K.u.k. Monarchy," which existed as a multi-ethnic state from 1867 until the end of World War I in 1918, had a substantial influence on present-day Austria. The monarchy was an extremely complex political entity, encompassing a variety of ethnicities and languages, including Germans, Hungarians, Czechs, Slovaks, Croats, Poles, Romanians, Ukrainians, and others. This led to a multitude of national and cultural identities within the empire, resulting in tensions and conflicts between the various ethnic groups. Despite its size and diversity, the monarchy was a significant political and economic power in Europe and played an important role in international relations. It experienced a period of economic prosperity and cultural advancement, particularly in urban centers such as Vienna and Budapest.

The linguistic landscape in Austria has also evolved over time. German is the official language of the country and is spoken by the majority of the population. However, there are also regional dialects and minority languages spoken in certain regions, such as

Burgenland Croatian, Slovene in Carinthia, and Hungarian in some communities in Burgenland. Austria is also home to a variety of ethnic minorities that enrich the country's cultural diversity. These include Hungarian, Slovenian, Croatian, and Czech minorities, which form historically established communities in various regions of Austria. Additionally, there is a growing number of people from other countries living and working in Austria, contributing to the country's cultural diversity.

Vienna: The Gateway to the Balkans and Eastern Europe- A Cultural Bridge between East and West

Vienna is not only the bustling capital of Austria but also serves as the gateway to the Balkans. The Iron Curtain, which divided Europe for decades, had a profound impact on Austrian society, particularly on Vienna. During the Cold War, Vienna was a neutral zone between East and West, a place of cultural exchange and espionage, but also a beacon of hope for many fleeing the communist regimes in Eastern Europe.

This history is still palpable in the streets of Vienna today, whether in the stories of older generations or in the memories preserved in museums and memorials. Eastern European culture has deeply woven itself into the daily life of Austria, especially in Vienna. Slavic and Hungarian names of shops and streets are part of Austrian culture due to history. The rich culinary diversity of the Balkans is reflected in the city's restaurants and markets, from hearty meat dishes to sweet pastry specialties. The Balkans are particularly prominent in Vienna's districts of Favoriten, Brigittenau, Hernals, Ottakring, and Leopoldstadt. Traditional dances and music from Eastern Europe are celebrated at street festivals and in dance halls, and art galleries showcase works by artists from the entire region. But the influence of the Balkans is not only felt in gastronomy and art. Diversity has also developed in architecture, language, and customs, making Vienna a true melting pot of cultures.

Economic Enchantment in Austria: Tradition Meets Innovation

Austria's economy boasts a rich history while simultaneously excelling in innovation and quality in the present day. The Austrian economy has its roots in a variety of industries ranging from traditional craftsmanship to high-tech sectors. Renowned for its top-notch quality and precision, Austria has a long tradition in areas such as mechanical engineering, automotive industry, metal processing, as well as food and beverage production. Small and medium-sized enterprises form the backbone of the economy and are often linked to generational traditions.

Today, Austria is primarily known for its flourishing export market, which ships a variety of products worldwide. From high-quality machinery and vehicles to specialties like chocolate and cheese, and even to luxurious watches and jewelry, Austrian products stand for quality, innovation, and reliability globally. Among the internationally renowned brands are Red Bull (energy drinks as well as sponsorship activities in extreme sports and entertainment), Manner (wafer specialties), Swarovski (high-quality crystal products and jewelry), voestalpine (steel and technology conglomerate), and OMV (international energy company).

Tourism also plays a crucial role in the Austrian economy, particularly in hospitality and gastronomy. With its breathtaking nature, historical landmarks, and top-notch leisure opportunities, Austria attracts millions of visitors from around the world each year. Austria has earned an excellent reputation internationally as a business location.

With a strong industrial base, a stable legal system, and a highly skilled workforce, Austria ranks among the leading countries in global competition. The country is known for its innovative spirit and strong export orientation, which have contributed to its establishment as an attractive investment location. In terms of gross domestic product (GDP), Austria is among the wealthier countries in the world, often ranking in the upper third in international comparisons. The average income per capita is also comparatively high, exceeding the EU average. Austria is part of the Eurozone and benefits from a stable currency and a solid economic structure. According to current data from the International Monetary Fund (IMF), Austria ranks among the top 30 countries in the world in terms of nominal GDP. This position underscores the economic strength and potential of the country in the global context.

Overall, Austria holds an outstanding position as a business location and continuously strives to strengthen its competitiveness and promote sustainable economic growth. To get an impression of Austria's economy firsthand, it is worth visiting companies yourself. Particularly worthwhile examples include the Swarovski Crystal Worlds in Wattens or the voestalpine Steel World in Linz.

Traveling in Austria: A Paradise for Explorers

How best to navigate through this diverse country, characterized by enchanting Alps, historic cities, and untouched nature? Let me give you insight into the wonderful world of Austrian transportation. Austria takes pride in its well-developed public transportation system, using Switzerland as a model. It allows travelers to journey comfortably and efficiently. The railway, with modern trains and high frequencies, is the star of interregional and regional travel, guiding you through picturesque landscapes. For those wishing to explore the beauty off the beaten path, regional buses provide an excellent opportunity to travel beyond the main routes.

In the bustling regional capitals such as Vienna, Salzburg, and Graz, excellent public transportation awaits, making it easy for you to explore the sights. Trams, commuter trains, buses, and subways quickly and conveniently take you from point A to point B. Austria is also well-connected for travel beyond its borders. While domestic air travel may be limited, international connections via air, rail, and road offer boundless opportunities to explore Europe. Vienna Airport serves as the international gateway to Austria. As the owner of a discount card, you benefit from attractive discounts on train travel, while weekends and holidays provide the perfect opportunity to take advantage of the public transit networks' affordable offers. With an inexpensive day ticket, you can travel to your heart's content through different regions of the country, making it ideal for day trips. For environmentally conscious travelers, Austria also offers a climate ticket valid year-round, allowing you to minimize your ecological footprint.

Besides public transport, Austria's road infrastructure offers very convenient and fast connections through the country with its offer of motorways.

Experiencing the Original Austria on the Farm

In Austria, the rural way of life and landscape have been shaped by agrarian structures for centuries. Agriculture is a crucial pillar of the economy, significantly contributing to the preservation of cultural landscapes and regional supply. The structure of agriculture in Austria is diverse, ranging from small family farms to larger agricultural enterprises. Traditional family farms still play a significant role, often closely intertwined with regional culture and identity. These farms often cultivate smaller plots and emphasize traditional farming methods and biodiversity. In recent years, the proportion of organic farming in Austria has increased significantly. Austria is considered a pioneer in organic farming, with organic products occupying a prominent place in supermarkets and farmers' markets nationwide. Many farmers have transitioned to organic farming to meet the growing consumer demand for sustainably produced food while also protecting the environment.

There are various types of farms in Austria, differing by region, topography, and tradition. These include dairy farms, pig and poultry farms, arable farms, fruit and wine-growing farms, as well as alpine farms. Each type of farm has its own characteristics and contributes in its own way to the diversity of Austrian agriculture. In addition to traditional farms, there is also a growing number of farm shops, direct marketing enterprises, and experience farms that offer visitors the opportunity to experience agriculture up close and purchase regional products. These enterprises play a crucial role in promoting rural tourism and strengthening regional value chains.

Vacationing on a farm is a unique opportunity to experience authentic Austrian country life while creating a wealth of unforgettable memories. What makes such a vacation so special? Well, it's the harmonious combination of nature, tradition, and hospitality that sets it apart. For families, especially those with children, a farm vacation is an outstanding choice. Here, children can discover nature in all its glory, experience animals up close, and learn the value of agricultural work. The opportunity to help out, whether feeding animals, milking cows, or harvesting, not only provides children with entertaining activities but also valuable learning experiences about responsibility and cooperation. There are numerous networks and organizations that allow travelers to actively participate in farm life. From official platforms listing farms welcoming guests (such as "Urlaub am Bauernhof") to local communities and events that promote interaction between farmers and visitors (such as "WWOOF"), there are many opportunities to experience this unique adventure. The hospitality of Austrian farmers is legendary. They open their doors and hearts to visitors, gladly sharing their knowledge and traditions. From cozy accommodations to delicious homemade meals, a stay on the farm offers a genuine sense of home and security.

So what can you expect when opting for a farm vacation? Apart from the picturesque landscapes and tranquility of country life, you can acquire a wealth of skills and knowledge. From baking bread to making cheese to gardening, there are many craft skills to learn from farmers. Additionally, a farm vacation provides a valuable opportunity to understand and appreciate the importance of sustainability and environmental protection. Overall, a farm vacation is an incomparable experience that not only refreshes the body and mind but also creates a deeper connection to nature and Austrian culture. It's a journey that enriches adventurers and tranquility seekers alike, creating unforgettable memories for the whole family.

The Melody of Austria: Classical Music and Its Heritage

Austria is renowned for its rich musical tradition, which has produced generations of composers and continues to touch the hearts of music lovers worldwide. From the majestic sounds of the Viennese Classical period to modern interpretations, the country offers a wealth of opportunities to experience classical music in all its glory. Salzburg, the birthplace of Wolfgang Amadeus Mozart, is considered the epicenter of classical music in Austria. The city practically breathes music history and is a pilgrimage site for classical music enthusiasts from around the world. The magnificent music festivals and concerts regularly held in Salzburg celebrate the legacy of Mozart and other significant composers in a magical way. The world-famous New Year's Concert of the Vienna Philharmonic is another highlight for music lovers in Austria. This annual event, broadcast live from the Golden Hall of the Vienna Musikverein, attracts visitors from around the world who seize the opportunity to welcome the new year with the enchanting sounds of the Strauss dynasty.

For tourists, it is entirely possible to attend concerts and events in Austria. A variety of tickets for music festivals, concerts, and opera performances can be purchased in advance online or at local ticket outlets. Many cities, including Vienna, Salzburg, and Graz, also offer special guided tours that take visitors to the most significant musical landmarks and provide insights into the country's rich musical history.

The Alpine Wonders of Austria: Nature Experiences in the Mountains

Austria takes pride in its breathtaking alpine landscapes, which provide an incomparable backdrop for outdoor activities and attract visitors from around the world. From majestic peaks to picturesque mountain villages, the country offers a wealth of opportunities to experience the beauty and tranquility of the mountains.

The Alps dominate Austria's landscape and offer a variety of activities for nature lovers and adventurers alike. Hiking is one of the most popular activities, allowing visitors to explore pristine nature, discover picturesque mountain lakes, and enjoy breathtaking views. In winter, the mountains transform into a paradise for skiers and snowboarders, with top-notch slopes and modern ski resorts suitable for everyone from beginners to professionals.

Mountain villages play an important role as recreational areas, providing visitors with the opportunity to experience traditional alpine life. Here, you can taste local specialties, purchase handmade souvenirs, and relax in cozy mountain huts while admiring the beauty of the surrounding landscape. Staying overnight in mountain huts adds a special flair; experiencing the sunrise or sunset on the mountain is unforgettable. Hut villages allow everyone to spend time close to the mountains in the midst of nature in both traditional and modern ways.

From Vienna, the Vienna Alps are easily and quickly accessible, offering a perfect escape from the hustle and bustle of the city. Popular destinations such as the Schneeberg and Rax offer a variety of hiking trails and viewpoints that are ideal for a day trip. A special experience here is the cogwheel train to the Schneeberg, shaped like a salamander.

Innsbruck holds a special position in the Alps, as it is not only surrounded by majestic peaks but also serves as a gateway to some of the world's best ski resorts. Stepping off the train or plane in Innsbruck, visitors are immediately impressed by the nearby mountains and peaks. The city is a popular starting point for outdoor adventures of all kinds and attracts visitors in both summer and winter who want to experience the beauty of the Alps up close.

The Viennese Coffeehouse Culture: A Delight for All Senses

The coffeehouse culture in Vienna is more than just a tradition - it's a way of life that has fascinated generations of locals and visitors alike. From elegant cafes to cozy pastry shops, the experience of coffee enjoyment in Vienna is an indispensable part of Austrian identity.

The history of coffee in Austria dates back to the 17th century when the first coffeehouses opened in Vienna. Since then, coffee enjoyment has become a staple of daily life, making Viennese coffeehouse culture a globally renowned phenomenon.

Austria ranks among the countries with high coffee consumption internationally. The love for coffee is deeply rooted in Austrian culture, and the variety of preparation methods and coffee specialties reflects the passion Austrians have for this beverage.

A visit to a traditional Viennese coffeehouse is a must for every visitor to the city. Places like Café Central, Café Sperl, and Café Hawelka are famous for their historic atmosphere, excellent service, and of course, their first-rate coffee. Here, you can linger for hours, read newspapers, people-watch, and enjoy the sweet idleness.

The waiters in Viennese coffeehouses play a crucial role in preserving the rich tradition of coffeehouse culture and significantly shape the guest experience. They are not just service staff but also ambassadors of this unique institution, characterized by their professionalism and Viennese charm. While not all guests may appreciate their distinct mentality, often interpreted as abrupt but well-intentioned, they have an excellent memory and can often recall the preferences and habits of their regular guests, leading to a particularly personalized service.

Another characteristic feature of Viennese waiters is their ability to engage in polished conversation. They are often well-informed about current events, cultural offerings, and, of course, the specialties of the house. This enables them to interact with guests in a pleasant and entertaining manner, creating a sense of connection.

In addition to coffeehouses, Viennese pastry shops are also worth a visit. Here, you can not only enjoy delicious coffee specialties but also sample a variety of traditional Austrian desserts such as Sachertorte, Apple Strudel, and Kaiserschmarrn.

Coffeehouses play a central role in the daily life of Austrians. They are not just places of enjoyment but also meeting points for friends, business partners, and families. Here, stories are exchanged, debates are held, and memories are created - all while holding a cup of delicious coffee.

Overall, Viennese coffeehouse culture is an indispensable part of Austria's cultural heritage and an experience that enchants and delights every visitor. Enjoy the ambiance of a coffeehouse and observe the scene - it's fascinating. A visit to a traditional coffeehouse is a journey into the past and an opportunity to experience the timeless elegance and unparalleled charm of this unique place.

Discovering Austria's Art Treasures: A Glimpse Behind the Scenes of Creative Masterpieces

Austria's artistic treasures are worth exploring, and no place offers such a rich array of art and museums as the charming capital city of Vienna. Begin your journey of discovery with the world-renowned art collections the city has to offer, including the magnificent Art History Museum and the fascinating Albertina.

The Art History Museum in Vienna is undoubtedly a jewel in the art world. With its breathtaking architecture and extensive collection of masterpieces from various epochs, it is a true treasure trove for art lovers. Be enchanted by the magnificent paintings of the Renaissance, the masterful works of the Baroque, and the fascinating sculptures. Famous paintings such as "The Art of Painting" by Johannes Vermeer and "The Flight into Egypt" by Pieter Bruegel the Elder are just some of the highlights this museum has to offer.

Located in the center of Vienna, in the vicinity of other significant buildings, the Albertina impresses with its diverse collection of graphics and drawings. Here, you can admire masterpieces by artists such as Albrecht Dürer, Rembrandt, and Michelangelo. In addition to the historical treasures, the Albertina also houses an impressive collection of modern art, including works by Picasso, Klimt, and Schiele. With its changing exhibitions and a wide range of artworks, the Albertina offers a fascinating journey through the history of art.

But that's just the beginning! Austria is dotted with other significant art museums waiting to be explored. The Belvedere Museum hosts an impressive collection of Austrian artworks, from Klimt to Schiele, while the Leopold Museum presents an extensive collection of Viennese Secession.

But wait, there's more! The Museum of Modern Art in Salzburg provides a fascinating insight into Austria's contemporary art scene, while the Lentos Art Museum in Linz captivates visitors with its innovative architecture and collection of modern art.

And who would have thought that some of these art pieces have also conquered the silver screen? The Belvedere Museum served as a backdrop for the iconic film "The Third Man," while the Leopold Museum was featured in "Before Sunrise," bringing Austria's art to life on the big screen.

Dance Enjoyment in Austria: From Traditional Steps to the Splendor of the Opera Ball

Immerse yourself in the world of dance in Austria, where the rich cultural tradition of dancing is alive and has been captivating people for centuries. For Austrians, dancing is more than just a leisure activity—it's an expression of joy, tradition, and community.

Austria's dance scene is closely intertwined with its classical music. Elegant steps of the Viennese waltz accompany countless events throughout the Alpine republic during the winter season. Whether it's the world-famous Opera Ball, the political party balls, the Confectioners' Ball, the Hunter's Ball, or the local Farmers' Ball—there's always something to celebrate in the enchanting ambiance, filling the night with dancing. Even during school, Austria's youth is almost unwittingly associated with classical dancing. Balls of higher education institutions (Matura ball) as a sort of expression of maturity, as well as later in university life, are commonplace and have always been very popular.

A highlight in the Austrian dance calendar is undoubtedly the famous Vienna Opera Ball. This glamorous event attracts celebrities, politicians, and dance enthusiasts from around the world every year to experience a night full of elegance, music, and dance. Debutantes are the young dancers who open the ball with a dance. Beneath the magnificent chandelier of the Vienna State Opera, guests whirl to the rhythm of the music and immerse themselves in the glamorous atmosphere of this legendary event. Generally, balls are considered public events, and anyone who manages to get a ticket is welcome to dance the night away.

Schönbrunn Palace: A Baroque Jewel with Imperial Splendor and Majestic Gardens

Vienna's Schönbrunn Palace, a true masterpiece of Baroque architecture, stands as a symbol of Austrian history. As one of Vienna's highlights, this UNESCO World Heritage Site attracts millions of visitors annually who fall in love with the magnificent halls and expansive gardens of the palace. Similar to the Palace of Versailles in France, Schönbrunn Palace is also a splendid example of royal residences built during the Baroque and Rococo periods.

Explore opulent rooms where Emperor Franz and Empress Sissi once resided. Immerse yourself in the fascinating world of the Austrian imperial family: from magnificent halls to intimate living quarters, Schönbrunn Palace offers a unique insight into the life and history of the Habsburg monarchy.

The vast palace gardens are a true paradise for nature lovers, providing an idyllic setting for leisurely walks and exploration. Stroll through intricately designed flower beds, wander along romantic avenues, and admire the majestic fountains and sculptures that adorn the gardens.

A visit to Schönbrunn Palace would not be complete without a stop at the famous palace café, where you can enjoy the royal atmosphere with a slice of Sachertorte and a cup of Viennese coffee. In short, a visit to Vienna without seeing Schönbrunn Palace cannot be considered a complete visit to Vienna.

Enjoyable Discovery Journey: Experience the Diversity of Austrian Cuisine

Austrian cuisine is characterized by its rich tradition, diverse flavors, and close connection to the country's history.

The origins of Austrian cuisine can be traced back to the time of the Habsburg Monarchy when royal chefs conjured up culinary masterpieces for the aristocratic rulers. This tradition of fine cuisine has evolved over the centuries and has become an integral part of Austrian identity.

A must-try for every visitor to Austria is the famous Wiener Schnitzel, golden-brown breaded and served with a slice of lemon. This delicious classic is a symbol of Viennese cuisine and is offered in practically every restaurant and 99.9% of the inns throughout the country.

Another sweet temptation is the world-famous Sachertorte, a creation of the Hotel Sacher in Vienna. This delicious chocolate cake with apricot jam and chocolate glaze is an absolute must-try for all dessert lovers and enthusiasts of traditional Austrian sweets. You can even have a piece of Sachertorte shipped home to you.

For dessert enthusiasts, Austria also offers the classic apple strudel, filled with apples, raisins, and cinnamon, as well as the irresistible Kaiserschmarrn, a fluffy pancake specialty sprinkled with powdered sugar and served with applesauce. It's worth noting that certain desserts are considered main courses by Austrians. Among the most common are the Kaiserschmarren and

Grießschmarren, Buchteln in vanilla sauce, the Scheiterhaufen, and Germknödel (also very typical in mountain huts in winter).

Among the many sweet temptations of Austrian cuisine, the Topfengulatsche and Punschkrapfen are true delights that you should definitely try as desserts or snacks.

The Topfengulatsche is a delicious pastry made from yeast dough, filled with a creamy quark mixture and often refined with raisins. It is a popular snack or sweet treat for coffee breaks. The combination of delicate dough and creamy filling makes the Topfengulatsche an irresistible delight for all sweet tooths.

On the other hand, the Punschkrapfen is a true Austrian delicacy that delights lovers of sweet pastries. This little masterpiece consists of airy sponge cake filled with a delicious rum punch filling and coated with pink sugar glaze. The sweet, slightly alcoholic taste of the Punschkrapfen makes it an unforgettable treat for anyone who tries it.

Both delicacies can be found in many Austrian bakeries and pastry shops and are loved by locals and visitors alike. A piece of Topfengulatsche or a Punschkrapfen are perfect companions for a cozy coffee break or a sweet souvenir to take home and savor the taste of Austria.

In addition to these famous specialties, Austria offers a variety of regional dishes and delicacies to discover, from hearty Kasnocken in Tyrol to savory Brettljause in Lower Austria and Styria.

The Magic of Summer Festivals

Welcome to a fascinating journey through the summer festivals of Austria, where music, theater, and art come to life in breathtaking settings, creating unforgettable experiences. These summer festivals are more than just events - they are cultural highlights that celebrate the diversity and creativity of Austria.

From the picturesque banks of the Danube in Melk to the majestic mountains of Reichenau an der Rax, these festivals provide a unique backdrop for cultural performances. The quality of the ensembles and productions is of the highest level, with talented artists and directors from around the world coming together to create magical moments on stage.

A highlight of the Austrian festival summer is the world-famous Bregenz Festival, which attracts thousands of visitors every year. These spectacular open-air performances on the Lake Constance stage offer unique productions of operas and musicals in a stunning setting that is unmatched.

The Salzburg Festival is undoubtedly one of the most famous and prestigious summer festivals in Austria and worldwide. Every summer, the picturesque city of Salzburg transforms into a stage for high-profile performances of operas, concerts, and plays. Founded in 1920, the Salzburg Festival has a long tradition and is known for its outstanding quality and artistic excellence. The performances take place at various venues in Salzburg, including the Festival Hall, the Felsenreitschule, and the Domplatz, with the city's baroque backdrop creating a magical atmosphere. The Salzburg Festival attracts renowned artists, conductors, directors, and ensembles from around the world who ensure first-class performances. From legendary conductors like Herbert von Karajan to international opera stars like Anna Netrebko, the Salzburg Festival has presented an impressive list of artists who have brought the stage to life with their talent and passion. The program of the Salzburg Festival includes a wide range of works from different eras and genres, with special emphasis on the performance of works by Mozart, who was born in Salzburg and is closely associated with the city. In addition to classical operas and concerts, the festival also presents contemporary pieces and innovative productions that delight and inspire the audience.

But even smaller festivals like the Erl Festival (in Tyrol) have their own charm and offer a diverse program of music, theater, and art. Here, visitors can feel the passion and dedication of the artists up close and enjoy unique cultural experiences. Since the demand for tickets to such events is usually very high, you should inquire in advance about ticket purchase options.

The Diversity of the Austrian Wine Landscape. Top Wines are the Norm!

As an Austrian wine enthusiast, I know that our country has a long tradition of winemaking and produces some of the best wines in the world. Begin your journey in Lower Austria, the largest wine-growing region in Austria, known for its diverse wine landscapes and excellent wines. From the picturesque Wachau to the sunny Weinviertel, you can enjoy a wealth of white wines like Grüner Veltliner and Riesling, as well as excellent red wines like Zweigelt and Blaufränkisch.

Burgenland in eastern Austria is also a world-renowned wine region, especially known for its robust red wines. The region around Lake Neusiedl produces unique sweet wines like the noble sweet Ruster Ausbruch and the world-famous sweet wine elixir, the Trockenbeerenauslese.

In Styria in southern Austria, you can discover the unique terroirs of the region and taste top-notch white wines like Sauvignon Blanc and Morillon (Chardonnay). Styria is also famous for its Schilcher wines, a vibrant rosé wine made from the Blauer Wildbacher grape.

Immerse yourself in the cozy atmosphere of Austrian Heurigen taverns, where you can enjoy regional specialties and fresh wines directly from the winemaker. The Heurigen culture is an integral part of Austrian lifestyle and offers a welcoming environment to taste local wines and meet locals. Heurigen calendars provide information about which Heuriger is currently open. Heurigen are not restaurants in the traditional sense; they are only open for a few weeks a year.

Along the Austrian Wine Road, you can participate in wine tastings along picturesque wine routes and discover the diversity of Austrian wines. From fruity white wines to robust red wines, Austria has something to offer for every wine lover. Moreover, Austrian wine is internationally exported (I've seen Austrian wine bottles in restaurants in Bali) and is known beyond national borders for its high quality and diversity.

Discover the Lifeline of Austria - the Danube

The Danube, Europe's second-longest river, meanders majestically through Austria and plays a crucial role in the history, culture, and economy of the country. But particularly fascinating is its stretch through the picturesque Wachau, a UNESCO World Heritage Site that enchants visitors with its beauty and diversity.

The Danube not only holds economic significance as a transportation route and a source of energy but also carries cultural importance reflected in the cities and villages along its banks. The Wachau, with its medieval castles, idyllic vineyards, and charming towns, is a perfect example of the unique culture thriving along the Danube.

A special highlight of the Danube in Austria is its role as part of the Rhine-Main-Danube Canal, which serves as an important link between the North Sea and the Black Sea. This waterway allows cargo ships to transport goods from Western Europe to the Eastern Mediterranean and is a significant factor in the trade and economy of the region.

The Wachau itself is a true gem along the Danube, famous for its picturesque wine villages, historic landmarks, and excellent gastronomy. You can cycle along the Danube (Danube Cycle Path), hike through the vineyards (Wachau World Heritage Trail), visit medieval castles, and of course, taste the delicious wines of the region.

Dürnstein is a picturesque town in the Wachau and plays a significant role in the region. The town is known for its charming medieval architecture, scenic location on the banks of the Danube, and rich history. A prominent landmark of Dürnstein is the ruin of Dürnstein Castle, which towers high above the town and offers breathtaking views of the surrounding countryside. This castle ruin is closely associated with the history of Richard the Lionheart, who was imprisoned here in the 12th century while returning from the Third Crusade. Legend has it that Richard the Lionheart was freed by a troubadour named Blondel de Nesle, who sang his song near the castle until he heard the voice of his king.

In addition to wine, a fruit plays a special role in the Wachau. The apricot, known as "Marille" in Austrian German, is a special variety of apricot and is considered a symbol of the Wachau. The region is famous for its delicious apricot products, including apricot jam, apricot schnapps, and of course, the famous apricot cake. The apricot blossom in spring is a breathtaking event that turns the landscape of the Wachau into a delicate pink and attracts numerous visitors. Apricots are not only an important harvest in the Wachau but also an essential part of the local culture and identity.

The "Goldhauben" are traditional head coverings worn in many parts of Austria, including the Wachau. They are a characteristic feature of the traditional costume culture and represent an important part of the region's cultural heritage. In the Wachau, the "Goldhauben" are often part of the traditional attire worn by women for festive occasions such as weddings, church fairs, and other traditional celebrations. These head coverings are often intricately decorated and embroidered with golden threads, giving them their name. They are worn along with other traditional costume elements such as dirndl dresses, aprons, and blouses.

As part of the UNESCO World Heritage Site, the Wachau offers a unique blend of natural beauty, cultural history, and culinary delights that attract visitors from all over the world. A boat trip on the Danube through the Wachau is an unforgettable experience and a perfect way to experience the beauty and diversity of this unique region. For example, it is recommended to take a boat from Krems to Dürnstein, Spitz, or Weissenkirchen and return by train.

Historical and Vibrant Gems Beyond Vienna

Apart from Vienna, the state capitals of Graz (Styria), Linz (Upper Austria), Innsbruck (Tyrol), and Salzburg (Salzburg) emerge as true treasures of architecture, tradition, and culture. Each city holds a hidden gem, yet they all share the same magnificent views.

Graz, the capital of the "green Styria," entices with medieval charm and a fascinating blend of history and modernity. Experience the vibrant heart of the city at Graz's Hauptplatz, where centuries of history converge. From the imposing Grazer Burg to the narrow lanes of the old town - Graz will enchant you with its charm. Clock Tower on Schlossberg: Enjoy a breathtaking view of Graz from the historic landmark Clock Tower on Schlossberg dating back to the 13th century. The sunset is particularly recommended when the city is bathed in golden light.

Our journey continues to Linz in Upper Austria, a city situated at the intersection of tradition and innovation on the banks of the Danube. Discover Linz's rich industrial past at Linzer Schloss and be inspired by the modern art scene at the Ars Electronica Center. Linz is a city that breathes history while looking towards the future. Take a ride on this historic tram and enjoy the panoramic view of Linz during the journey to Pöstlingberg: perfect for a relaxed afternoon stroll or coffee enjoyment in one of the charming cafes.

Salzburg, the city of music and festivals, welcomes you with baroque splendor and an aura of romantic elegance. Stroll through the picturesque alleys of the old town, a UNESCO World Heritage Site, and admire the majestic Mirabell Palace. Salzburg will seduce you with its timeless beauty. A true hidden gem is the Gaisberg. Escape the hustle and bustle of the city and take a hike up

Gaisberg. From here, you'll have a breathtaking view of Salzburg and the surrounding mountains.

Finally, our journey leads us to Innsbruck, the capital of the Alps. Surrounded by stunning mountain scenery, Innsbruck combines history and nature in a unique way. Marvel at the Golden Roof, the city's landmark, and experience Tyrolean hospitality in the traditional parlors of the old town. Experience the fascination of ski jumping up close at this modern ski jump on Bergisel, which has always been a fixed part of the Four Hills Tournament for ski jumping. In addition to the adrenaline rush, the viewing platform offers a spectacular view over Innsbruck and the surrounding mountain landscape.

Traditions and Customs That Touch the Heart

There are countless festivals and customs celebrated on a large scale in Austria, and you can be right in the midst of them. Let's start with the grandest celebration, which illuminates Austria in a very special bright light. Christmas in Austria is a very special festival, characterized by a rich cultural tradition and a warm, festive atmosphere. Austria is rich in traditional customs and rituals that shape the Christmas celebration. These include lighting the Advent wreath, setting up the Christmas tree, singing Christmas carols, and visiting Christmas markets. The Christmas markets in Austria are globally renowned for their unique atmosphere and traditional craftsmanship. Cities and villages across the country transform into festively decorated markets where you can buy handmade gifts, try traditional foods, and enjoy mulled wine. Christmas in Austria is characterized by a contemplative mood where people spend time with their families, exchange gifts, and adhere to traditional values such as charity and community spirit. Austrian Christmas cuisine is rich in delicious specialties that make the festival a culinary highlight. These include gingerbread, stollen, vanilla crescents, Christmas cookies, and, of course, the traditional Christmas roast. In addition to the Christmas markets, Austria hosts a variety of special events during the Christmas season, such as Advent concerts, nativity plays, festive opera and ballet performances, and traditional Christmas Eve Masses in churches. The snowy landscapes of Austria lend a fairytale atmosphere to the Christmas season. The picturesque mountains, forests, and lakes provide an idyllic backdrop for the festival and invite you to winter walks and outdoor activities.

Fasching (Carnival) in Austria is a time of exuberant celebrations and colorful traditions that bring people of all ages together. Austrian carnival processions are known for their creative costumes, colorful floats, and captivating music. Costumes and floats are crafted and decorated in months-long preparations, usually at the club or community level. Carnival time is also known for its opulent balls, as well as the previously mentioned Opera Ball.

Local fire brigade festivals are an important tradition in Austria and serve several purposes. On the one hand, they are an opportunity for local fire brigades to present themselves to the community and honor their work. On the other hand, they offer locals and visitors the chance to meet, celebrate, and have fun together. Fire brigades use their festivals as additional sources of income, as these events are mostly organized voluntarily. Traditional foods and drinks are served to celebrate local cuisine and pamper visitors. Beer as well as grilled chicken or sausage, as well as cakes and live music (preferably by a brass band), are essential elements of fire brigade festivals. Fire brigade festivals are usually held over three days, from Friday to Sunday. A Sunday lunch at the local fire brigade festival by the surrounding population is tradition, but every guest is welcome! The announcement of fire brigade festivals is typically indicated by posters along the country roads.

The summer solstice is traditionally celebrated in Austria on June 21st and marks the longest day and shortest night of the year. This centuries-old celebration has deep roots in Austrian culture and is often associated with mystical rituals and festivities. People gather at special locations such as mountain peaks to watch the sunset and honor the power of the sun. Fires are lit to symbolize the sun. Insider tip: in the Wachau region, countless fires are lit along the Danube, which can be wonderfully seen from the ships.

Kirtage are traditional folk festivals held in many Austrian villages and towns in the summer. They are often associated with religious celebrations dedicated to the local church or a particular saint. Kirtage offer a wealth of activities for the whole family, including fairground attractions, live music, dancing, culinary delights, and much more.

Furthermore, regional folk festivals (usually held annually) are multi-day events based mainly on agriculture, forestry, and livestock farming. In addition to exhibition opportunities in these areas, amusement parks offer a welcome change from everyday life for the population in the region.

The Glorious History of the Babenbergers and Habsburgs

The Babenbergers, one of the most significant ruling dynasties of medieval Austria, left behind a rich cultural and architectural heritage that continues to shape the country to this day. As the first dukes and margraves of Austria, they played a decisive role in shaping the land and its identity.

The Babenberg dynasty, named after their progenitor Babo of Bavaria, ruled over Austria from around 976 until the year 1246. Their influence extended far beyond the borders of the country and encompassed large parts of present-day Germany and Austria.

Culturally, the Babenbergers were significant patrons of art and culture. They erected magnificent churches, monasteries, and castles that still stand today as witnesses to their power and splendor. Among the most famous buildings of the Babenberg era is the Melk Abbey Church, a masterpiece of baroque architecture that played a significant role in the intellectual and cultural life of the Middle Ages.

The Babenbergers also left their mark on literature and the visual arts. They supported the development of Middle High German poetry and promoted the dissemination of manuscripts and books in their territories. Moreover, they were patrons of artists and craftsmen involved in the design of their magnificent residences and castles.

From an architectural standpoint, the Babenbergers shaped the landscape of Austria with imposing castles and fortresses that served as symbols of their power and influence. Among the most famous structures are Krems Castle, Wiener Neustadt Castle, and Hardegg Castle, which are regarded as symbols of Babenberger rule over the land.

The Habsburgs, one of the most significant dynasties in Europe, left a rich cultural and architectural legacy in Austria that continues to shape the country to this day. For centuries, the Habsburgs ruled over Austria, not only shaping the political landscape but also the art, culture, and architecture of the country.

As one of Europe's most powerful ruling families, the Habsburgs promoted the arts and sciences and contributed to Austria's development as a cultural center. They were significant patrons of artists, musicians, and writers, thus creating a flourishing cultural scene that is still palpable today.

Architecturally, the Habsburgs are especially known for their magnificent palaces and residences. Among the most famous are the Hofburg and Schönbrunn Palace in Vienna, both of which are UNESCO World Heritage Sites and among the most visited attractions in Austria. These magnificent buildings testify to the power and wealth of the Habsburgs and are symbols of imperial grandeur and the splendor of bygone eras.

Furthermore, the Habsburgs also left behind a rich cultural legacy in the form of art collections, libraries, and museums. The art collections of the Habsburgs, including the Picture Gallery of the Academy of Fine Arts in Vienna and the Art History Museums in Vienna and Graz, house some of Europe's most significant art treasures and are an impressive legacy of their cultural preferences and interests.

Skifahren ist das Leiwandste

... (translated as "Skiing is the best thing ever") as sung by the Austrian pop musician Wolfgang Ambros, reflecting the Austrian sportsman's soul. Skiing is more than just a sport for us Austrians - it is a passion, a part of our culture. From the majestic peaks of the Alps to the snowy valleys, we offer ski enthusiasts an unparalleled experience.

Our national heroes in skiing are legends like Hermann Maier and Marcel Hirscher, who have impressed the world with their incredible performances. Their victories and winning mentality have not only conquered our country but also the hearts of all ski fans.

In our schools, ski weeks are an integral part of the curriculum. Children are introduced to skiing at an early age and learn not only the technique but also respect for the mountains and nature. Skiing also has a significant social component, as ski weeks strengthen the sense of community.

Austria is globally renowned for its excellent ski resorts and top-notch slopes. From the legendary Arlberg to the cozy Tyrolean Zugspitzarena - our diversity leaves nothing to be desired. And don't forget the cozy mountain huts, where you can enjoy traditional Austrian cuisine during your ski day or afterwards, ranging from Kaaspressknödelsuppe to Wiener Schnitzel and Berner Würstel to Germknödel.

A ski vacation in Austria is something truly special. It's the combination of perfectly groomed slopes, breathtaking mountain scenery, and warm hospitality that makes it unique. Here, you experience the magic of winter in its purest form.

Away from the ski slopes, Austria offers a wealth of other winter sports opportunities that will thrill every adventurer. From breathtaking cross-country skiing through snowy forests to the thrill of snowboarding in deep powder - there is something for everyone here. For those who prefer a more leisurely pace, winter hikes or snowshoeing are excellent ways to explore the untouched nature and enjoy the silence of the snowy landscape. Real adrenaline junkies can try ice climbing or race down steep slopes with a snowbike. And of course, we must not forget the traditional sports like ice skating, sledding, and curling, which are practiced in many places. Whatever winter sport you choose, in Austria, you'll find the perfect conditions and a warm, welcoming atmosphere that will make your winter vacation unforgettable. So pack your gear and get ready for a winter adventure in the Austrian mountains - the fun of your life awaits!

So, strap on your skis and dive into the skiing pleasure of Austria. Experience the freedom on the slopes, feel the wind on your face, and let yourself be enchanted by the magic of the mountains. Welcome to the ski nation of Austria - here awaits the adventure of your life!

The Best Slopes and Legendary Mountain Slopes

Immerse yourself in the world of Austrian ski resorts, where tradition meets modernity and the slopes are as diverse as our landscapes. From the snow-covered glaciers to the sunny slopes, we offer everything a skier's heart desires.

In Tyrol, Salzburg, and Vorarlberg, you'll find some of Austria's most famous ski resorts. Tyrol entices with tradition and charm in places like St. Anton am Arlberg and Kitzbühel, while the Salzburg Alps score with modern facilities in Zell am See and Saalbach-Hinterglemm. Vorarlberg delights with its internationally renowned ski resort in the Arlberg region. For snow-sure adventures, the glacier areas in Tyrol and Salzburg offer ideal conditions, while in Carinthia and Styria, sun worshippers among the skiers feel at home. Here too, you'll find a variety of slopes and slopes that have something to offer for every skier. Modern ski resorts include places like Ischgl in Tyrol, known for its vibrant nightlife and innovative lifts, as well as the futuristic ski resort Sölden in the Ötztal Valley, which also serves as a venue for World Cup races. One of the last James Bond films, "Spectre," was filmed in the Austrian Alps, including the Sölden ski resort in the Ötztal Valley. But no matter which ski resort you choose, one thing is for sure: in Austria, you'll experience skiing like nowhere else. So, grab your skis or your snowboard and get ready for unforgettable descents, breathtaking views, and the warm hospitality of our mountain villages. On your marks, get set, go!

Unbroken Football Fever in Austria

In Austria, football is more than just a sport - it's a passion deeply rooted in our culture. On one side, there are the traditional clubs like Rapid Vienna, Vienna, and Austria Vienna, which have been winning the hearts of football fans for many decades. Their history, rivalries, and loyal supporters make them true legends of Austrian football. Viennese derbies between Rapid Vienna and Austria Vienna are among the true highlights of sporting events in Austria.

On the other side stands Red Bull Salzburg, a modern and innovative club that sets new standards with its financial backing, focus on youth, and international orientation. Although they may face criticism, they have significantly shaped Austrian football in recent years, gained international recognition, and reached new heights.

The fan culture in Austria is vibrant and diverse. From the enthusiastic supporters who cheer for their teams at every game to the spectacular choreographies and chants - the stadium experience is unique and unforgettable. Crowd pullers include home games of Rapid Vienna, Sturm Graz, and Red Bull Salzburg.

The Austrian national football team has had a chequered history, but in recent years, it has developed into a solid and competitive team. With talented players, most of whom earn their living abroad, a solid squad is available to provide surprises at major events such as the European Championship and the World Cup. Although their greatest successes are many years ago (3rd place in Switzerland), the team receives great support from the

Austrian population, especially at their home games in the national stadium (Ernst Happel Stadium in Vienna).

In Austria, there are over a thousand football clubs, ranging from the Bundesliga down to the regional leagues. Almost every place or village has its own football pitch and club. Whether big or small, every club has its own history and heroes who make up the heart of football in Austria. Currently, the most well-known active Austrian football stars include David Alaba (Real Madrid), Marko Arnautovic (Inter Milan), and Marcel Sabitzer (Borussia Dortmund).

Hallstatt as the Hidden Jewel in the Alps

Hallstatt is a place like no other - nestled between majestic mountains and the glittering Hallstätter Lake. Its picturesque beauty and rich history attract tourists from all over the world. The history of Hallstatt dates back several thousand years and is closely linked to the salt mine, which has been in operation since antiquity. The salt from Hallstatt was once invaluable and brought wealth and prosperity to the area. Numerous archaeological finds testify to the early settlement and cultural richness of the region.

Over the centuries, Hallstatt has been shaped by various rulers and cultures, including the Celts, the Romans, and the Habsburgs. Today, the town is a UNESCO World Heritage Site. Hallstatt is particularly popular among nature lovers, hikers, and photographers who want to explore the breathtaking landscape and picturesque half-timbered houses. Culture enthusiasts also get their money's worth because Hallstatt is rich in historical attractions such as the ossuary and the salt mine.

However, the fame of Hallstatt also has its downsides. The popularity of Hallstatt has brought problems such as overcrowding and environmental pollution, especially during the high season. Therefore, it is advisable to visit Hallstatt during the quieter months to be able to enjoy the atmosphere and beauty of the place in peace. The Chinese copy of Hallstatt in the Guangdong province has caused a stir and raises questions about cultural identity and authenticity.

Away from the hustle and bustle, the surroundings of Hallstatt offer a variety of activities and attractions. From boat trips on the lake to hikes through the surrounding mountains - there is something for everyone to discover. One of the most famous mountains is the Dachstein, which attracts hikers and climbers from all over the world with its impressive peaks and breathtaking views. From Hallstatt, you can easily reach the summit with the Dachstein-Krippenstein cable car and enjoy the spectacular landscape. Another worthwhile destination is the Hoher Dachstein, the highest mountain in the region and a paradise for mountaineers and climbers. From its peak, you have a breathtaking view over the entire region and even as far as Slovenia.

Austria's stages stand for theater, opera, and much more!

In Austria, cultural life pulsates on the stages - from classical theater plays to opulent operas, and from captivating musicals to light-hearted operettas. Here you will find a rich tradition and a vibrant scene that will delight every art lover.

The history of stage culture in Austria dates back a long way and is marked by great names like Mozart, Schubert, and Strauss. Their works have conquered the stages of the world and still shape the repertoire of many theaters, concert halls, and opera houses today.

Among the most famous stars of Austrian stage art are artists like Anna Netrebko, Elīna Garanča, and Jonas Kaufmann, who enchant audiences with their extraordinary voices and interpretations. The most prestigious stages and ensembles in Austria include the Vienna State Opera, the Burgtheater in Vienna, and the Salzburg Festival. These venues are considered the best and most beautiful in the country and offer a first-class program for every taste.

Some of the most well-known and respected theater actors in Austria today include Klaus Maria Brandauer, Birgit Minichmayr, Cornelius Obonya, Maria Happel, and Nicholas Ofczarek.

But outstanding events are not limited to the classical realm - Austria also has a lot to offer in the field of concert events. Festivals like the Donauinselfest in Vienna, the Frequency Festival in St. Pölten, the Nova Rock in the Pannonia Fields, and the Electric Love

Festival in Salzburg attract thousands of music fans from all over the world every year and provide unforgettable experiences.

The Donauinselfest is undoubtedly one of the largest and most popular festivals in Europe - and the best part? Admission is completely free! The festival takes place over three days and offers a diverse program for every taste. On multiple stages along the Danube Island, local and international artists from the genres of pop, rock, electronic, hip-hop, and more perform. From established stars to up-and-coming talents, there is something here for everyone to discover.

Soak up untouched nature in Austria's national parks

Austria's national parks are true treasures of nature, created to protect and preserve the diversity and beauty of our landscapes. They provide unique habitats for rare plants and animals and are havens for relaxation seekers and nature lovers. In total, Austria's six national parks cover an area of almost 2,400 km2. The national parks include the Gesäuse National Park in Styria; Hohe Tauern National Park in Salzburg, Tyrol, and Carinthia; Kalkalpen National Park in Upper Austria; Neusiedler See-Seewinkel National Park in Burgenland; Thayatal National Park in Lower Austria; and Donau-Auen National Park in Lower Austria and Vienna.

One of Austria's most famous national parks is Hohe Tauern National Park. With its imposing peaks, deep valleys, and untouched forests, it is the heart of the Alps and a paradise for hikers, mountaineers, and naturalists. Another outstanding national park is Gesäuse National Park in Styria. Here, spectacular rock formations meet wild and romantic river valleys, offering a unique experience for outdoor enthusiasts and adventurers. The Donau-Auen National Park, located near Vienna, stretches along the Danube and is an important habitat for rare animal and plant species. With its wet meadows, floodplain forests, and river landscapes, it offers a unique backdrop for nature lovers and bird watchers.

Austria's national parks are not only havens for nature but also places of relaxation and adventure for visitors from all over the world. Here, you can experience the untouched beauty of nature, discover rare animals and plants, and enjoy the silence of the mountains and forests. The best way to explore the national parks is with hiking boots; marked hiking trails help ensure you don't miss any highlights.

On the trail of noble steeds

Horses play a significant role in Austrian history. From the noble stables of the Habsburgs to the proud Lipizzaners that adorned royal courts, horses have shaped Austria's cultural heritage.

In Austria, around 450,000 horses gallop across green pastures and picturesque landscapes. An impressive number that shows how deeply rooted Austrians' love for their horses is. In addition to the Lipizzaner, there are other horse breeds typical of Austria, such as the Haflinger. These robust and versatile horses originate from the Alpine regions of Tyrol and South Tyrol. They are known for their friendly nature, endurance, and strength. Furthermore, there are the Norikers, which are indispensable in the Austrian horse landscape. Norikers are an ancient Austrian working horse breed known for their sturdy build and versatility. They are often used in traditional costume festivals and historical events. Pinzgauers originate from the Pinzgau region in Salzburg. They are medium-sized, robust, and known for their endurance and agility, making them good working and leisure horses.

The Lipizzaners, one of the oldest horse breeds in the world, are the jewel of Austrian horse breeding. Their elegance, grace, and exceptional dressage abilities make them global ambassadors for Austrian equestrian art. The Spanish Riding School in Vienna is a Mecca for horse lovers. Here, you can experience the legendary Lipizzaners in action and admire their breathtaking dressage skills that have fascinated people around the world for centuries.

Dreaming of an unforgettable horse adventure in Austria? Then saddle up and discover the picturesque riding trails and idyllic landscapes of the Alpine country. Whether in Salzburg, Styria, or

Carinthia - here you will find the perfect place for your horse holiday. "Farm holidays" are particularly suitable for this, and high-quality family hotels also offer horseback riding holidays on their premises.

Christmas in Austria

Servus! The pre-Christmas season in Austria is a true celebration for all the senses. Here you will discover which Advent markets you should definitely visit and what awaits you there. Advent markets are temporary huts built in a rustic style, often arranged in a circle. At the Advent markets in Austria, you will find an abundance of handcrafted gifts and regional delicacies. Locals as well as tourists enjoy the culinary offerings outdoors and are enchanted by the glow of the lights.

From traditional Christmas ornaments to intricate ceramics, and from delicious gingerbread to mulled wine - there is something for everyone here. Let yourself be inspired by the variety of offerings and find unique souvenirs for your loved ones. Advent markets are usually located in large squares such as the Rathausplatz. In larger cities, these markets are open daily during Advent and usually close on Christmas Eve. Smaller villages organize Advent markets only on weekends during the Christmas season. There is no admission fee, but tips and donations are very much appreciated during this serene time. Some of the most famous Advent markets in Austria include:

Wiener Christkindlmarkt at Rathausplatz: Immerse yourself in the enchanting atmosphere in front of the magnificent Vienna City Hall. Here you will find traditional craftsmanship, delicious treats, and a diverse entertainment program.

Salzburger Christkindlmarkt at Domplatz: Against the backdrop of the imposing Salzburg Cathedral, you will experience the magical atmosphere of the pre-Christmas season here. Stroll through the winding alleys, enjoy mulled wine, and discover handcrafted gifts.

Graz Adventmarkt at Hauptplatz: The largest Advent market in Styria entices with its diverse range of arts and crafts, regional specialties, and atmospheric music. Here you can fully enjoy the pre-Christmas atmosphere.

Adventure Playground Austria

Austria's nature has a lot to offer, and you shouldn't miss out on it. Here are the top 5 nature experiences you absolutely must have on your trip:

Hohe Tauern National Park: Attention, summit seekers!

Dive into the breathtaking mountain world of Austria's largest national park. Here, majestic peaks, crystal-clear mountain lakes, and untouched nature await you. Venture on hikes through wild canyons and discover the diversity of alpine flora and fauna.

Donau Auen: Nature idyll along the Danube

Explore the untouched wetland landscapes along the Danube and experience the unique flora and fauna of this exceptional ecosystem. Paddle through winding river arms, observe rare bird species, and relax amidst the tranquil nature.

Krimml Waterfalls: Natural spectacle in the Alps

Impressive masses of water plunge here into the depths (380 m height difference) and form Europe's highest waterfalls. Experience the thundering roar of the Krimml Waterfalls, feel the refreshing spray on your skin, and enjoy the sight of this imposing natural wonder.

Green Lake: Diving adventure in the Styrian Alps

The Green Lake in Styrian Tragöß is a jewel of nature. In spring, when snow and ice melt, the lake transforms into a turquoise-green oasis. Dive into this clear water and discover a fascinating underwater world full of mysterious rock formations and plants.

Neusiedler See (Lake Neusiedl): Nature paradise in eastern Austria

Discover the unique landscape of Lake Neusiedl, one of the largest steppe lakes in Europe. Here, you can observe water birds, cycle through idyllic vineyards, or sail on the water. Enjoy the peace and expansiveness of this special region. The lake invites you to windsurf and sail to a special degree. In addition, cycling and hiking trails offer varied insights into the special landscape around Lake Neusiedl. Tip: Don't forget your passport as Lake Neusiedl also includes Hungary. You can immerse yourself in two different cultures on a day trip.

Ready for unforgettable nature experiences in Austria? Pack your hiking shoes, grab your camera, and explore the diversity of Austrian landscapes. Unforgettable adventures await you!

Tracing Austrian History

Austrian literature has a long and rich history, marked by significant works and talented authors. Austrian literature traces its roots far back in time. From the epic works of the Middle Ages to the modern literature of the 21st century, it has dealt with a variety of themes, including love, identity, society, and politics.

Austrian authors have grappled with a variety of themes reflecting human life and society. These include the quest for identity, processing wartime experiences, the relationship with nature, and the examination of societal norms and values.

Austria can be proud of its Nobel laureates in literature. Famous names like Elfriede Jelinek, Peter Handke, and Elias Canetti have shaped world literature with their works. But many other Austrian authors, such as Arthur Schnitzler, Franz Kafka (born in Prague but of Austrian origin), and Robert Musil, have gained international fame. The year 2024 is particularly marked by Kafka's legacy, as it marks the centenary of his death.

Whether classics or contemporary works, Austrian literature has something to offer for every taste. Dive into the fascinating world of Arthur Schnitzler's psychological novels, experience the disturbing intensity of Elfriede Jelinek's works, or discover the timeless wisdom of Thomas Bernhard's prose.

In cities like Vienna, Salzburg, and Graz, there are museums and memorials dedicated to famous Austrian writers. Here, you can learn more about their lives, works, and their influence on literary history. Some cities offer special guided tours focusing on the literary history and favorite spots of writers. During such tours, you can discover the city from the perspective of its literary residents. Look out for literary events like readings, book presentations, or literature festivals taking place during your stay. These offer a great opportunity to meet contemporary Austrian authors and connect with other literature enthusiasts.

Pure relaxation!

The thermal bath culture in Austria is more than just a trend – it's part of our way of life. The tradition of thermal baths in Austria dates back to the time of the Romans. Even then, the healing properties of warm thermal water were valued and utilized. Today, you can experience this heritage in numerous modern thermal baths throughout the country.

Thermal water is rich in minerals and trace elements that can have positive effects on health. It alleviates muscle and joint pain, promotes circulation, strengthens the immune system, and relaxes the body and mind. In addition to the health benefits, a visit to the thermal bath also offers a welcome break from everyday life. Enjoy the pleasant warmth of the water, relax in the various pools, and leave the stress behind.

Sauna culture also has a long tradition in Austria. In most thermal baths, there is a variety of saunas to suit every taste – from the classic Finnish sauna to steam baths and herbal saunas. Typically, in Austria, the sauna area is entered nude. Equipped with a bath towel and slippers, you enter the sauna area to comply with hygiene rules. The bath towel is used as a seat cover and during the infusion itself to circulate the air. A cold shower or ice bath afterwards will revive your spirits.

In the last two decades, thermal culture in Austria has evolved significantly. Modern thermal baths not only offer top-notch wellness and health facilities but also an extensive leisure and entertainment program for the whole family. The high-quality standards of the guests are completely fulfilled.

Thermal resorts are easy to find on the map in Austria, as they usually begin with the prefix "Bad" (meaning "bath"). Among the best-known of the approximately 40 thermal resorts are Baden near Vienna, Bad Hofgastein, Bad Blumau, Bad Gleichenberg, Bad Waltersdorf, and so on.

Pack your swimwear and experience pure relaxation and rejuvenation amidst the picturesque Austrian landscape!

Experience Austria through its personalities: Insights into the lives of famous Austrians

Immerse yourself in the fascinating world of renowned figures who have shaped Austria – both in their lifetimes and beyond. From legendary artists like Mozart and Klimt to visionary thinkers like Freud and Schrödinger – they have all enriched the world with their work and shaped Austria's cultural landscape.

Discover the workplaces of these icons, known far beyond Austria's borders. Visit the Mozarthaus in Salzburg, where the genius's sound still resonates, or stroll through the magnificent halls of the Vienna Secession, where Klimt's masterful works ignite the senses.

But it's not just in art; Austrians have also achieved greatness in science. Follow in the footsteps of Sigmund Freud in Vienna, where his groundbreaking theories still shape psychology today, or explore the University of Vienna, where Erwin Schrödinger researched the fundamentals of quantum physics.

Even modern heroes of Austria deserve our admiration. From sports legends like Niki Lauda, whose courage and perseverance remain unforgettable, to political figures like Bruno Kreisky, who led the country through turbulent times – their stories inspire and encourage us to give our best.

While Austria proudly looks back on its outstanding personalities, there are also those who are mistakenly associated with the country. One such case is Adolf Hitler, who, although born in Austria, is known as a German dictator. In contrast, Ludwig van

Beethoven is often mistakenly considered Austrian, despite being born in Bonn, Germany.

Be inspired by the diversity and heritage of these extraordinary individuals and delve into the soul of Austria. Behind every landmark and sight lies a fascinating story – and who better to tell it than the people who have made Austria what it is today? Their passion, their visions, and their legacy continue to shape the face of our country, making Austria a place full of inspiration and cultural diversity.

The Myth of Sisi

Sisi, actually Elisabeth of Austria, was a true legend in our parts. The empress, known for her breathtaking beauty and unconventional lifestyle, still exerts a strong fascination on people today.

Her life resembles a fairy tale, albeit one with many dark sides. As empress, she was surrounded by luxury and splendor on the one hand, but restricted by strict etiquette rules and the constraints of the Viennese court on the other. Sisi longed for freedom and individuality, which was unusual and often rebellious for an empress of her time.

Her close connection to Austria is evident especially in the magnificent imperial palaces like Schönbrunn and the Hofburg in Vienna. Here, one can experience the aura and splendor she created around herself. But even away from the imperial court, there are places closely linked to her life. For example, the Achensee area in Tyrol, where she liked to spend her time and where traces of her can still be found today. Or the Hungarian city of Gödöllö, where she had one of her summer residences and where one can still feel the grandeur of past times.

Sisi's tragic end, her death by assassination, only intensified the myth surrounding her. She became an icon of romance and the yearning for freedom that still touches the hearts of people today.

To better understand the myth of Sisi, I recommend following in her footsteps through Austria. Her story is full of drama, love, and passion, and there are many places and monuments (notably those in Vienna, Salzburg, and Bad Ischl) that remind us of her.

Immerse yourself in the world of the empress and let yourself be enchanted by her fascinating personality.

Austria's Sommerfrische: A Tradition of Relaxation and Rejuvenation!

The Sommerfrische has a long-standing tradition here. Originally stemming from the time of the Austro-Hungarian Empire, affluent city dwellers, particularly from Vienna, sought to escape the hot city life and spend the summer months in the cooler mountains. They sought relaxation, fresh air, and nature.

During this time, they lived in magnificent villas and hotels in the mountains or on the shores of lakes, where they enjoyed the summer months. These villas were often luxuriously furnished, offering every conceivable comfort, from fine dining to elegant social events.

Today, the Sommerfrische has evolved somewhat, but the core idea remains intact. It still revolves around escaping urban hustle and bustle, enjoying nature, and rejuvenating. Many people spend their summer vacations in the Austrian Alps, by the lakes, or in thermal spa regions, where they hike, swim, or simply soak in the idyllic landscape.

Well-known places closely associated with the concept of Sommerfrische include the regions around Lake Wolfgang, Lake Attersee, or Lake Traunsee in Upper Austria, as well as the Salzkammergut or the Tyrolean Alps. So, if you want to escape the summer heat and truly take a break from everyday life, Sommerfrische in Austria is just the thing for you!

Masterpieces of Engineering

Austria is famous for its impressive engineering achievements that impress both tourists and locals alike. One of the first and most well-known examples is the Semmering Railway. This historic railway line runs through the picturesque landscape of the Semmering Pass. Built between 1848 and 1854, it is an outstanding example of early railway construction. The Semmering Railway was the first mountain railway in the world that could be traversed by a steam-powered locomotive. Its construction was highly demanding as it had to overcome steep gradients, tight curves, and deep valleys. To accomplish this, numerous technical innovations were employed, including the famous Semmering System, where massive stone walls were built to protect against avalanches and rockfalls. The Semmering Railway was declared a UNESCO World Heritage Site in 1998 and is still in use today as an active railway line between Vienna and Graz.

Another technical masterpiece is the Grossglockner High Alpine Road. This breathtaking panoramic road winds through the Austrian Alps and offers spectacular views of Austria's highest mountain, the Grossglockner (3,798m). Along the Grossglockner High Alpine Road and in the surrounding areas of the Austrian Alps, there is a rich population of marmots. These charming rodents inhabit the alpine meadows and rocks and can often be spotted along the road. Built in the 1930s, the road remains one of the country's most popular tourist attractions.

Another impressive structure is the Danube Island in Vienna. This artificially created island stretches along the Danube River and offers numerous recreational opportunities, including bike paths, parks, and beaches. The Danube Island is a remarkable example of

Austrian engineering and urban planning and showcases its best side every summer with the Danube Island Festival.

Furthermore, Austria is known for its numerous historical castles and fortresses, which often exhibit impressive architectural and technical features. These include, for example, Schönbrunn Palace in Vienna, Hohensalzburg Fortress in Salzburg, and Hochosterwitz Castle in Carinthia.

Action!

Welcome to the world of Austrian cinema, a rich source of artistic expression and captivating stories! From iconic classics to modern masterpieces, Austria has produced a diverse film tradition that is recognized worldwide.

While the Austrian film industry may be small, it is extremely vibrant and innovative. Austrian filmmakers are known for their creative approach and their ability to bring profound themes to the screen. With its diversity and talent, the Austrian film scene has secured a solid place on the international stage.

Some of the most well-known Austrian films include works like "The Counterfeiters" (2007) by Stefan Ruzowitzky, which won an Oscar for Best Foreign Language Film, as well as "Funny Games" (1997) and "The White Ribbon" (2009) by Michael Haneke, both award-winning works known for their intense and provocative portrayal of human life.

Austria offers a wealth of picturesque locations that attract filmmakers from around the world. The majestic Alps, historical cities, and idyllic landscapes of the country often serve as backdrops for films of all genres. For example, scenes from the famous film "The Sound of Music" (1965) were shot in the scenic region around Salzburg, making this area a popular destination for film fans.

Austria has also produced a number of talented actors who have achieved success both nationally and internationally. Among them are legends like Romy Schneider, Klaus Maria Brandauer,

Christoph Waltz, and Arnold Schwarzenegger, who captivate audiences with their impressive performances and charisma.

Arnold Schwarzenegger, globally known as an action hero and former Governor of California, has his roots in Austria. Born in Thal, a small village in Styria, Schwarzenegger grew up in modest circumstances, but his relentless ambition and unwavering determination to pursue his dreams led him to an unparalleled career. Schwarzenegger initially gained fame as a bodybuilder, winning numerous titles, including the coveted Mr. Olympia competition. However, his hunger for success knew no bounds, and he eventually conquered the silver screen with his distinctive presence and charismatic demeanor. Films like "Terminator," "Predator," and "Total Recall" made him one of the biggest action stars of the 1980s and 1990s. Despite his international success, Schwarzenegger never forgot his connection to his homeland of Austria. He has consistently been involved in charitable efforts in Austria and represented his country as an ambassador around the world. His journey from a small village in Styria to a globally renowned superstar is an inspiring example of the American dream and a symbol of the success that can be achieved through hard work and determination. Arnold Schwarzenegger will always remain a source of Austrian pride, having captured the hearts of people in his homeland and around the world.

Austria can be proud of its Oscar winners, who have represented the country on the international stage. In addition to Stefan Ruzowitzky, who won the Oscar for "The Counterfeiters," Michael Haneke and Christoph Waltz have also been honored with the coveted trophies, acknowledging their significant contributions to the art of cinema.

Experience up close!

The history of zoos in Austria dates back to the 18th century when the first menageries were established to showcase exotic animals from distant lands. Since then, zoos have evolved into important educational and recreational facilities that advocate for the protection and preservation of endangered species. Many zoos in Austria are also involved in research and conservation projects, contributing to raising awareness about environmental and species conservation issues. By visiting a zoo, you can not only discover the fascinating world of animals but also contribute to the preservation of our natural habitats.

From historical zoos to modern wildlife parks, Austria offers an impressive selection of places where you can experience nature up close. One of the most famous zoos in Austria is undoubtedly Tiergarten Schönbrunn in Vienna, the oldest existing zoo in the world. Since its founding in 1752, Tiergarten Schönbrunn has attracted countless visitors and offers an impressive variety of animal species in a beautiful historical setting.

Another well-known zoo is Zoo Salzburg, located in the heart of the city and home to a variety of exotic animals. The Tierpark Hellbrunn near Salzburg is also worth a visit, offering not only an impressive array of wildlife but also historical water features and gardens.

Away from the well-known tourist destinations, Austria also has a number of zoos that are less known but still impressive. One example is the Alpenzoo Innsbruck, specializing in the wildlife of the Alpine region and presenting a unique collection of alpine animals. The Wildpark Ernstbrunn in the Weinviertel region is also worth a visit, offering the opportunity to observe native wildlife in a natural habitat. Tierpark Rosegg in Carinthia is another gem, specializing in endangered species and advocating for biodiversity conservation.

Modern masterpieces and their creators

Immerse yourself in the fascinating world of Austrian architecture, where traditional craftsmanship meets innovative designs. From historical buildings to modern skyscrapers, Austria's architecture shapes the skyline and cultural heritage of the country. Below are some highlights worth taking a closer look at.

The renowned Austrian architect Wolf D. Prix, together with Helmut Swiczinsky and Michael Holzer, founded the architectural firm "Coop Himmelb(l)au." Their most famous work is the Haas House in Vienna, an iconic building located on Stephansplatz known for its futuristic architecture and daring glass facade.

The internationally acclaimed architect Zaha Hadid also left her mark in Austria. Her project, the Kunsthaus Graz, is a striking example of contemporary architecture. The futuristic building, also known as the "Friendly Alien," houses modern art exhibitions and attracts visitors from around the world.

Hermann Kaufmann is considered a pioneer of modern timber construction. His sustainable and innovative wood structures shape the Austrian architectural scene. An outstanding example of his work is the HoHo Vienna, a multi-story wood hybrid building in Vienna, which is considered one of the tallest timber high-rises in the world.

The Hundertwasser House, designed by Friedensreich Hundertwasser, is a colorful and imaginative residential building in Vienna's third district. With its distinctive facade and organic forms, it has become a landmark of the city, attracting visitors from around the world.

The Ars Electronica Center in Linz, designed by the architectural firm Treusch Architecture, is a futuristic building dedicated to the intersection of art, technology, and society. With interactive exhibitions and events, it offers insights into the world of digital culture and innovation.

Last but not least, the Gasometers in Vienna, also known as Gasometer City, deserve mention. They are an impressive example of transforming industrial structures into modern residential and commercial centers. The four massive gas tanks have been converted into apartments, offices, shops, and recreational facilities, shaping the city's skyline today.

Museums as treasure troves of culture

The Austrian art market is vibrant and diverse, with a range of established galleries, auction houses (such as "Dorotheum"), and art fairs regularly showcasing artworks by Austrian and international artists. Vienna is a significant center for the art trade, hosting a variety of galleries and art dealers offering a wide range of artworks, from historical masterpieces to contemporary works.

Overall, Austria offers a rich cultural landscape that attracts art lovers from around the world and provides plenty of opportunities to explore and enjoy the world of art. From renowned museums to small galleries, there is something to discover and experience for every taste and interest.

Among the most famous museums in Austria is the Albertina in Vienna. The Albertina, one of Austria's leading art museums, houses an impressive collection of graphics, drawings, and prints from various periods. In addition to its permanent collection, the Albertina regularly hosts high-profile special exhibitions on various themes and artists.

The Kunsthistorisches Museum, one of the most significant art museums in the world, displays an extensive collection of paintings, sculptures, and art objects from various periods and cultures. Highlights include works by Rembrandt, Vermeer, Rubens, and many other masters of art history.

Another notable museum is the Mumok in Vienna. The Museum of Modern Art Foundation Ludwig Vienna (Mumok) is the leading museum for contemporary art in Austria. It presents an extensive collection of works of modern and contemporary art, including paintings, sculptures, photographs, and multimedia installations.

In addition to the major museums, Austria also has a vibrant scene of galleries and exhibition spaces that regularly organize smaller vernissages and exhibitions. These events provide artists with the opportunity to showcase their works to a broad audience and allow visitors to discover new talents and interact with the artists.

Natural Beauties for Relaxation and Enjoyment

Austria's lake landscape is unparalleled. From idyllic bathing lakes to majestic reservoirs, Austria offers a variety of opportunities to enjoy the clear water and fresh air.

In terms of bathing lakes, Carinthia offers the largest selection. Lake Wörthersee is one of the most famous and popular lakes in Austria. With its clear, turquoise-blue water and picturesque shores, it provides ideal conditions for swimming, sunbathing, and water sports. The charming towns around the lake invite you to linger and offer a variety of leisure activities.

Lake Ossiach is another popular bathing lake in Austria. With its shallow shores and warm water, it is particularly suitable for families with children. In addition to swimming, there are also numerous water sports activities such as sailing, windsurfing, and diving.

Lake Millstatt is characterized by its crystal-clear water and surrounding mountains. It is a popular destination for nature lovers and offers a variety of hiking and cycling trails along its shores. Here too, picturesque towns invite you to linger and offer a wide range of leisure activities.

Lake Neusiedl, located on the border between Austria and Hungary, is the largest steppe lake in Central Europe and a UNESCO World Heritage Site. With its shallow shores and shallow water, it is a paradise for waterfowl and offers ideal conditions for sailing, windsurfing, and kitesurfing.

The Salzkammergut region in Austria is known for its stunning landscape, which includes a variety of picturesque lakes. Here are some of the most remarkable lakes in the Salzkammergut. Lake Wolfgangsee is one of the most famous lakes in the Salzkammergut and attracts visitors with its clear water and surrounding mountains. The lake is ideal for swimming, boating, and walking along its promenades. The towns of St. Wolfgang, St. Gilgen, and Abersee offer charming places to enjoy the beauty of the lake.

Lake Mondsee is another picturesque lake in the Salzkammergut, known for its idyllic location and clear water. The lake offers numerous water sports opportunities such as sailing, windsurfing, and swimming. Along the shore of the lake are charming villages like Mondsee and St. Lorenz, which invite you to linger and explore.

Furthermore, Lake Attersee is the largest lake in the Salzkammergut and known for its crystal-clear water and surrounding mountains. The lake is a popular destination for water sports enthusiasts and offers ideal conditions for sailing, windsurfing, and diving. The towns of Unterach, Nußdorf, and Steinbach am Attersee offer opportunities to relax and enjoy the picturesque landscape.

Lastly, Lake Hallstatt is famous for the picturesque village of Hallstatt, located on its shores and surrounded by steep mountains. The lake provides a stunning backdrop for boat trips and walks along its promenades. The UNESCO World Heritage Site of Hallstatt and the surrounding areas invite exploration and discovery.

Additionally, Austria is known for its countless smaller lakes in the form of reservoirs and gravel pits. The residents of the surrounding areas enjoy the cool water during the hot summer months just a few minutes' bike ride from their doorstep. Barbecue and camping facilities make the lake adventure an unforgettable experience.

Experience Graz: Insider Tips and Must-Sees

Hey, welcome to Graz! This city is full of surprises and has something to offer for everyone. Here's what you definitely shouldn't miss, and a few hidden gems you should definitely discover. Despite its age (founded in the 12th century), the city is considered a popular regional metropolis and thrives due to its large student population. With approximately 300,000 inhabitants, the capital of the state of Styria marks the second largest city in Austria.

When you're in Graz, there are a few things you absolutely must see. The Kunsthaus Graz is a true architectural gem and a must-visit for art lovers. Then, of course, there's the Schlossberg - climb it for a breathtaking view over the city and discover the history of the fortress. The Old Town is listed as a UNESCO World Heritage Site, and Graz was also the European Capital of Culture in 2003.

But don't just be impressed by the main attractions. Immerse yourself in the Griesviertel, a real neighborhood with local cafes and shops, off the beaten path. Or take a stroll through the Augartenpark, a hidden gem of nature in the middle of the city.

And don't forget to explore the Kunsttunnel Graz - an underground tunnel adorned with fascinating street art. Here you'll find creative artworks and plenty of inspiration.

In terms of sports, Graz is closely connected to the local football clubs SK Sturm Graz and Grazer Athletiksport Klub (GAK). Founded in 1909 and 1902 respectively, there is a lively rivalry between these clubs, both of which have celebrated Austrian football championship titles in the past and have also made waves on the international stage.

Austria's Contribution to the European Capitals of Culture

Austria has a rich history and tradition in the cultural development of Europe and has made significant contributions to the European Capitals of Culture over the years. These titles are awarded by the European Union to celebrate the cultural heritage and diversity of Europe and to promote exchange between people. The Austrian European Capitals of Culture have left a lasting impact on the cultural landscape of the country. So far, Austria has made three contributions to the European Capitals of Culture:

In 2003, Graz, together with the Slovenian city of Maribor, was the European Capital of Culture. Under the motto "People - Places - Times," Graz presented a wide range of cultural events, exhibitions, and projects that highlighted the city's diversity and creativity. The events ranged from music and theater performances to art installations and intercultural encounters. The Murinsel is a direct legacy from this time.

In 2009, Linz was the European Capital of Culture and used this title to present itself as a center for art, culture, and innovation. Under the motto "Linz changes," numerous projects and events were organized that enriched the city's cultural life and showcased the diversity of its cultural scene. The highlight was the opening of the Ars Electronica Center, a center for digital art and media art, which has since become an important attraction for artists and visitors from around the world. The Ars Electronica Center (an interactive museum for digital art and media art) is one of the city's main attractions and has developed into an internationally renowned center for digital culture since its opening.

In 2024, Bad Ischl, along with its immediate surroundings (Salzkammergut with 23 municipalities in Upper Austria and Styria), represents Austria's contribution to the European Capital of Culture. With its variety of diverse locations and events, it is definitely worth visiting this part of Austria.

Cultural Treasures to Discover

Austria is characterized by its multitude of monasteries and abbeys. Each one has its own unique history, architecture, and cultural significance, taking visitors on a fascinating journey into the past. From magnificent Baroque buildings to medieval treasures, they offer a variety of cultural and spiritual experiences that make every visit unforgettable. If one wishes to delve deeper into the fascination of these special places, the following five are recommended for a visit:

Perched high above the Danube, Melk Abbey is one of the most beautiful Baroque monasteries in Europe. Its magnificent architecture, lavish interiors, and impressive library make it a unique cultural gem. Visitors can explore the Baroque gardens and enjoy the splendid view of the Danube.

Also known as the "Austrian Monte Cassino," Göttweig Abbey impresses with its imposing location on a hill overlooking the Wachau Valley. The Baroque monastery complex houses a rich collection of artworks and precious books. A highlight is the magnificent abbey church with its golden decorations. From the abbey, one can marvelously overlook the Danube, the vineyards of the Wachau and Kremstal regions, as well as the city of Krems.

Located in Styria, Admont Abbey is the largest monastery in Austria and impresses with its impressive library, which is considered one of the most beautiful in the world. The magnificent ceiling frescoes, Baroque architecture, and intricate stucco work make the abbey a fascinating cultural destination. Due to its proximity to Gesäuse National Park, it is ideal to combine a visit to the abbey with a hike.

Klosterneuburg Abbey (12 km northwest of Vienna) is a significant monastery and one of the oldest abbey complexes in Austria. Particularly impressive is the abbey church with its Romanesque and Gothic elements, as well as the collection of medieval art treasures.

Last but not least, mention must be made of Heiligenkreuz Abbey, a Cistercian monastery in Lower Austria. It is famous for its Gregorian chants and its long tradition as a spiritual center. The Gothic abbey church and the idyllic location in the Vienna Woods make it a special place of tranquility and contemplation.

Cultural Highlights Known Across Borders

The Salzburg and Bregenz Festivals are among Austria's most prestigious cultural events and are known far beyond the country's borders. These festivals offer a rich program of music, theater, and opera annually. The Salzburg and Bregenz Festivals are not only cultural highlights for Austria but also significant cultural ambassadors that showcase the country's artistic heritage on the international stage. They contribute significantly to Austria's cultural diversity and reputation as a major cultural hub in Europe.

The Salzburg Festival has been held every summer in the picturesque city of Salzburg since 1920, the birthplace of Wolfgang Amadeus Mozart. The festival attracts opera lovers, theater enthusiasts, and music fans alike, offering performances by world-class artists in unique historical settings, including the famous Hohensalzburg Fortress and the Festspielhaus. The Salzburg Festival stands for the highest artistic quality and presents a diverse program of operas, concerts, plays, and readings every year. The performances are curated by renowned directors, conductors, and performers, offering an unparalleled cultural experience for visitors from around the world. The play "Everyman" (Jedermann) serves as a flagship, performed annually. Written by Hugo von Hofmannsthal, it addresses life, death, and the transience of humanity in the format of a mystery play.

The Bregenz Festival has been held on the shores of the picturesque Lake Constance in Bregenz (Vorarlberg) since 1946 and is especially known for its spectacular lake stage productions. The breathtaking natural backdrop of Lake Constance serves as the unique stage for impressive productions of operas, musicals, and concerts. The highlight of the Bregenz Festival is the production held every few years on the famous lake stage, which attracts worldwide attention with its monumental stage sets and spectacular effects. The combination of first-class music, impressive staging, and picturesque landscape makes the Bregenz Festival an unforgettable cultural experience for visitors of all ages.

Exploring Nature's Treasures in Austria's UNESCO Biosphere Reserves

Austria takes pride in its six UNESCO Biosphere Reserves, which serve as protected areas for the environment while offering unique natural landscapes to explore. These reserves encompass a wide range of ecosystems and are home to a variety of plant and animal species, inviting visitors to engage in various activities.

The Wienerwald Biosphere Reserve spans the Wiener Basin and offers a rich diversity of habitats, including forests, meadows, and historic villages. Here, you can enjoy numerous outdoor activities such as hiking, cycling, and birdwatching.

In Carinthia, the Nockberge Biosphere Reserve is known for its gentle alpine meadows and striking mountain peaks. As a hiker and mountaineer, you can explore the breathtaking landscape here and discover rare plant and animal species.

In the Großes Walsertal in Vorarlberg, the Großes Walsertal Biosphere Reserve stretches across a traditional cultural landscape with green valleys and idyllic alpine villages. Sustainable agriculture and tourism projects harmonize with nature here.

The Lungau Biosphere Reserve in Salzburg provides habitat for a variety of rare animal species and is a popular destination for outdoor enthusiasts. Here, you can experience untouched nature while hiking, skiing, and observing wildlife.

In Upper Austria, the Kalkalpen Biosphere Reserve is characterized by steep rock walls and dense forests. Adventurous individuals like you can climb, mountain bike, and explore the unique wildlife here.

For nature lovers and outdoor enthusiasts, the Karwendel Biosphere Reserve (in Tyrol and Bavaria) offers a wealth of activities, including hiking, climbing, mountain biking, and wildlife observation. Well-marked hiking trails and huts invite you to enjoy the pristine nature and breathtaking views of the surrounding mountain peaks.

Winter Wonderland

The SkiWelt Wilder Kaiser-Brixental is an absolute paradise for skiers and snowboarders. It is one of the largest and most diverse ski areas in the world, offering an incredible selection of slopes and runs for every skill level and preference.

Here, you can enjoy more than 284 kilometers of excellently groomed slopes, from gentle beginner slopes to challenging steep descents. With over 90 ski lifts, you can quickly and comfortably reach the peaks, where breathtaking views await you.

What makes SkiWelt special is also the unique panoramic landscape surrounding the majestic Wilder Kaiser and the Kitzbühel Alps. The snow-covered peaks, picturesque valleys, and cozy mountain villages create a magical atmosphere that makes every day of skiing an unforgettable experience.

In addition to skiing, there are also numerous opportunities for winter activities such as sledding, cross-country skiing, and winter hiking. The cozy mountain huts and restaurants invite you to linger and pamper you with delicious regional specialties and après-ski.

Castles as Witnesses of a Rich History

Austria is rich in castles, not for nothing is the state named Burgenland. They are not only impressive architectural masterpieces but also living witnesses of a turbulent past. Below, I would like to list some of the most famous castles that are worth visiting and exploring.

The medieval Hohenwerfen Castle in Salzburg majestically overlooks the Salzach Valley and offers a fascinating insight into medieval life. Highlights include the well-preserved fortress with its imposing towers and walls, the historical armory, and the spectacular falconry demonstrations that take visitors into the fascinating world of falconry.

Kreuzenstein Castle (just a stone's throw from Vienna) is one of Austria's most impressive castles and is considered one of the most beautiful castles in Europe. The highlight of this castle is undoubtedly its unique architecture, which is a mixture of medieval ruins and reconstructed elements from the Renaissance and Baroque periods. Visitors can explore the magnificent interior, admire the rich collection of historical artifacts, and take a glimpse into the past. The castle is also known for its birds of prey show and served as a backdrop for the 2011 Hollywood film "Season of the Witch."

Hohensalzburg Castle is one of the largest and best-preserved medieval castles in Europe, majestically dominating the skyline of Salzburg. The highlight of this castle is undoubtedly the breathtaking view that stretches from the battlements of the fortress over the city and the surrounding landscape. Visitors can explore the imposing defensive structures, visit the historical rooms, and participate in fascinating tours to learn more about the castle's turbulent history.

Riegersburg Castle is an impressive fortress that towers high above the gentle hills of the South Styrian vineyards. The highlight of this castle is its imposing architecture, characterized by massive walls, mighty towers, and an impressive location. Visitors can explore the impressive defensive structures, visit the historical armories, and listen to fascinating stories about the castle's past. A special highlight is the view from the castle's towers, which offers a breathtaking panoramic view of the picturesque landscape of Styria.

Salt as a precious resource then and now

Salt has played a significant role in Austria's history. Since ancient times, salt has been a valuable commodity used not only for seasoning food but also as a preservative and for ritual purposes. Austria boasts rich salt deposits that have been mined for centuries, shaping the country's economy significantly.

Salzburg, whose name is derived from the Latin "sal" (salt), owes its wealth to the salt trade. The city was a crucial hub for salt, evolving into a center for salt mining and trade. Today, numerous attractions such as the Salzburg Salt Mine and the Salt Museum commemorate the importance of salt to the city's history.

The picturesque village of Hallstatt in the Salzkammergut has been known for its salt mining for over 7,000 years. The salt mines of Hallstatt are among the oldest in the world and are a UNESCO World Heritage Site. Visitors can tour the historic salt mines and learn more about the history of salt mining in the region.

The Salzburg Lake District (including Wolfgangsee and Mondsee) offers not only picturesque landscapes and crystal-clear waters but also a rich history of salt mining. Mondsee and Wolfgangsee were once important locations for salt trading and are now popular destinations for water sports and relaxation.

Although salt mining in Austria no longer holds the economic significance it once did, salt remains an important raw material and plays a role in modern industry, particularly in food production and chemistry. Visitors can explore the topic of salt in museums, exhibitions, and experiential environments, where they can learn more about the history, extraction, and uses of this precious mineral. Additionally, guided tours of historical salt mines offer the opportunity to explore the fascinating underground world of salt extraction. One of the most spectacular salt experiential environments is the Hallstatt Salt Mine in the Salzkammergut. This visitor mine offers a fascinating journey into the world of salt mining, the history of the region, and the significance of salt. Visitors have the opportunity to venture deep into the mountain and explore the underground tunnels and passages, while learning intriguing stories about the lives of miners and working conditions in the salt mine. A particular highlight is the ride on the mine railway deep into the heart of the mountain.

Top 5 Day Trips from Vienna

Vienna may be a fascinating city, but sometimes it's nice to escape the hustle and bustle of the big city and explore the beauty of the Austrian countryside. From idyllic lakes and imposing castles to magnificent monasteries and majestic mountains, Austria offers plenty of opportunities for exciting day trips. Here are the top 5 day-trips from Vienna that will take you to the hidden treasures of the country and provide unforgettable experiences. All are easily accessible from Vienna by either rental car or public transportation.

Lunz am See is an idyllic village nestled in the stunning nature of the Mostviertel region. The picturesque Lunzer See invites relaxation and enjoyment, whether swimming, boating, or simply strolling along the shore. The Urwald (primeval forest) near Lunz am See is a unique natural gem in Austria. As one of the last primeval forests in Central Europe, it offers an unparalleled insight into the natural development of a forest ecosystem that has remained virtually untouched for centuries. This forest is home to a wealth of plant and animal species, including rare and endangered species that are scarcely found in other parts of Europe. Hiking trails lead through this pristine forest area, creating a fairytale atmosphere with its dense tree canopies, moss-covered tree trunks, and picturesque streams.

Burg Kreuzenstein is an imposing medieval castle perched high above the hills of Lower Austria. The castle impresses with its fascinating architecture and offers breathtaking views over the surrounding landscape. Visitors can explore the historic rooms, participate in a birds of prey show, and immerse themselves in the fascinating world of the Middle Ages.

Stift Melk is an architectural masterpiece and a jewel of the Baroque era. The magnificent abbey majestically overlooks the Danube and impresses with its opulent interiors, artistic frescoes, and splendid libraries. A visit to the abbey not only provides insight into the rich history and culture of the region but also offers an unforgettable view of the picturesque Danube landscape.

Lake Neusiedl is a paradise for nature lovers and water sports enthusiasts. The shallow lake is ideal for sailing, windsurfing, and kitesurfing and also offers numerous opportunities for swimming and relaxing on the beach. The surrounding region is also known for its picturesque vineyards and cozy wine villages, which invite you to wine tastings and culinary experiences.

The Schneeberg is the highest mountain in Lower Austria and a popular destination for hikers and nature lovers. With its distinctive shape and diverse flora and fauna, the Schneeberg offers numerous hiking opportunities for all skill levels. A special highlight is the ride on the cogwheel train (designed like a salamander) to the summit, from where you can enjoy breathtaking views of the Alpine landscape.

Other highlights for day trips include the Marchfeld castles (Marchfelder Schlösser) and the Wachau region.

Austria as a Global Stage

Austria plays a significant role on the global stage through its membership in various international organizations. These organizations cover a wide range of areas, from economics and trade to peace and security. Here are some of the most important international organizations represented in Austria, and the neutral role the country plays in these organizations.

The United Nations (UN) is the foremost international organization for cooperation and diplomacy, with its headquarters in New York. In Austria, the UN is represented through various offices and organizations, including the United Nations Office at Vienna (UNOV) and the International Atomic Energy Agency (IAEA). Austria plays an active role in UN bodies and advocates for peace, security, and development on a global scale.

The OECD (Organization for Economic Cooperation and Development) is an organization focusing on economic cooperation and development, headquartered in Paris. Austria is a member of the OECD and actively participates in the organization's policy discussions and programs. As a highly developed economy, Austria plays an important role in shaping international economic and social policies.

The OPEC (Organization of the Petroleum Exporting Countries) is an international organization of oil-exporting countries, headquartered in Vienna. Although Austria is not an oil-exporting country, Vienna serves as the headquarters of the organization and a venue for important conferences and negotiations. As a neutral country, Austria provides an ideal setting for diplomatic discussions and international cooperation in the energy sector.

Austria's neutral role in these and other international organizations makes the country an important player on the global stage and contributes to the promotion of peace, stability, and economic development.

ABOUT THE AUTHOR

Dieter J. F. Haselsteiner is a father of three kids, husband and passionate writer who is a native of Austria. He loves to travel, read and write books, spending time in the nature by going hiking and skiing. Additionally, Dieter is an aviation enthusiast and published seven books so far. With this publication, Dieter dedicates his passion about his home country in the form of culture and travel insights.

Imprint

Publisher: Dieter Haselsteiner

Diesendorf 24

3243 St. Leonhard am Forst

AUSTRIA

ISBN: 9798327466746

Self-published – printed by Amazon Kindle Direct Publishing

The front-cover is based on original photos provided by Mr. Colo, Rene Bittner, Julius Silver, Thomas Wolter, Julie Kolibrie, and Sekau67.

Printed in Great Britain
by Amazon